With God...
on a
Tanzanian Safari

to Kaeleigh,

Annette Friesen Cone

With God...
on a
Tanzanian Safari

Annette Friesen Cone

JUST DUST PUBLISHERS

Just Dust Publishers
1025 NE Irvine Street
McMinnville, OR 97128
Office@JustDustPublishers.com
JustDustPublishers.com

© 2014 by Just Dust Publishers
All rights reserved. Published 2014
No part of this book, neither text nor photos,
may be reproduced in any manner without permission
from the publisher. To obtain consent, contact:
office@JustDustPublishers.com
Printed in the United States of America
First paperback edition, 2014
ISBN: 978-0-9838333-8-3

Scripture quotations taken from:
The New American Standard Bible (NASB), ©1995
by The Lockman Foundation
Used by permission. (www.Lockman.org)

Scripture quotations marked (NLT) are taken from:
The Holy Bible, New Living Translation, ©2013
by Tyndale House Foundation
Used by permission of Tyndale House Publishers, Inc.
Carol Stream, Illinois 60188
All rights reserved.

Scripture quotations marked (AMP) are taken from:
The Amplified Bible, ©1987
by The Lockman Foundation
Used by permission. (www.Lockman.org)

Photographs: Annette Cone & Abigail Cone
Photograph on page 45: Fulgence Kennedy
Cover Design & Interior Layout: Matthew Dollinger

Preface

In early May of 2014, I had an amazing safari adventure in Tanzania, along with my husband and our 21 year old daughter. While I do admit straightforwardly that I am no expert on anything African, safari or otherwise, God did speak to me in the experience, and my inspiration was confirmed in His Word.

Our safari guide took us to Tarangire, Manyara, Ngorogoro Crater, and Serengeti National Parks.

What follows are my observations and biblical passages that came to mind and heart during that special time in Tanzania, Africa. Please join me, dear Reader, in a short African devotional with God's Word as our safari guide.

~Annette Friesen Cone

~1~
Masks

For now we see in a mirror dimly,
but then face to face;
Now I know in part,
but then I will know fully
just as I also have been fully known.
1 Corinthians 13:12 (NASB)

I felt like dancing on our first day of safari. After a restful night's sleep in our comfortable hotel in Arusha, my husband, daughter, and I met our driver and guide, Willy, and set off on the drive to Tarangire National Park. Just before the park entrance, Willy pulled over for a rest stop and a chance to see some woodcarvers as they fashioned souvenirs in a little shack behind a shop that was surrounded by grazing goats in the fields.

Three men sat on low benches with tools and chunks of wood in hand. Some of their finished pieces, a tall giraffe figurine and carved masks, were grouped together in a corner on the dirt floor. These men were true artists, evidenced by the intricacy of their carvings.

I was hoping to find African artwork to grace my guest room wall at home, and so chose a pair of slender carved masks, one a giraffe, the other a zebra. Both were stained in natural earthy colors, etched with black lines that highlighted each one's beautiful features. Zebras and giraffes are two of my favorite animals, and I knew the masks would remind me of their beauty and grace.

Once a chunk of wood from a tree, my Tanzanian masks were not intended to be worn or to hide a face, as masks normally do. Instead, they were created with pure beauty in mind. I like to touch the backside of my masks, fingering the artist's tool marks from his labor of carving, and imagine his painstaking attention to detail and the time it took him to create my masks.

Think of yourself as a mask. You are a beautiful work of art, and God has created your life with a purpose in His mind. He chips away what is eternally useless and artfully paints colors that highlight forever-features of glory as only He can do.

My African masks are beautiful on my guest room wall. They are an artist's interpretation of the graceful giraffe and zebra. But God's unveiling of His most masterful creations—you and I—will be more beautiful than any earthly expression or art form.

But we all, with unveiled face,
beholding as in a mirror the glory of the Lord,
are being transformed into the same image
from glory to glory,
just as from the Lord, the Spirit.
2 Corinthians 3:18 (NASB)

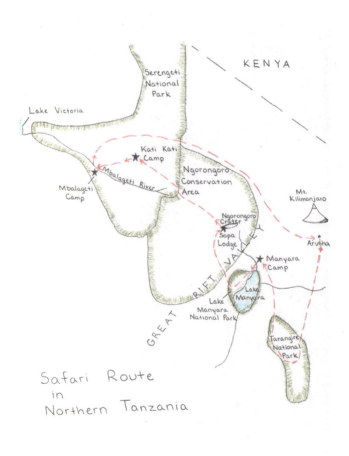

Map: Phoebe Cone, Abigail Cone & Annette Friesen Cone

~2~
Swahili Sounds

The words of the LORD are pure words;
as silver...
Psalm 12:6a (NASB)

Language is so interesting. I love to study Hebrew and Greek meanings as I read my Bible. I even enjoy the sounds of other languages: the fluidity of French, the musicality of the Scandinavian dialects, and the soft lilt of southern Asian island nations.

In Tanzania, the Swahili words written on signs are written with the letters I know in the alphabet. But some of the sounds are different. I especially like a consonant sound that 'leans upon' another consonant. This is not the same as a consonant 'blend,' because one letter is dominant, and the other is complimentary. To pronounce Ngorogoro (the beautiful volcanic crater park) and Mbalageti (a camp and river in the Western Serengeti), one must only hint at the beginning "N" and the second letter "b," respectively. And so, if you said, "Gorogoro" and "Malageti," you wouldn't be too far off in correct pronunciation. But the beauty in the spoken names Ngorogoro and Mbalageti are a joy to hear. Try saying them out loud to yourself—go ahead, be brave!

Now I think of God's wonderful words. It's not just the sounds that make these words special, though I love to read them aloud. These words in my Bible are "living words." They reach deep into my soul, comforting me and showing me the best way to live.

These words tell the story of God's lovingkindness through the ages. They are words that are personal, written for me from my heavenly Father. Each time I read them, I notice something new, and this is what makes them alive: they are infused by the Spirit of God as He speaks to my spirit through His written word. God teaches, challenges, and encourages me with these words. I am so thankful for them! I remember a song we sang when I was a child: "Sing them over again to me, wonderful words of life. Let me more of their beauty see, wonderful words of life. Words of grace and beauty; Teach me faith and duty; Beautiful words, wonderful words, wonderful words of life."

The law of the LORD is perfect,
restoring the soul...
They are more desirable than gold,
yes, than much fine gold;
Sweeter also than honey
and the drippings of the honeycomb.

Psalm 19:7a, 10 (NASB)

~3~
Chameleon Eyes

*The eyes of the LORD search the whole earth
in order to strengthen those
whose hearts are fully committed to Him.*
2 Chronicles 16:9a (NLT)

On the second day of safari, our jeep bumping along a gravelly road, our driver, Willy, stopped quite suddenly. Without a word, he stepped out of the jeep, walked to the middle of the road, picked up a bright green lizard, and carefully set it on a big rock off to the side of the road. We followed him, curious by his action.

As my family gathered around the rock to listen to his discourse about the chameleon, I was fascinated by the chameleon's eyes. With each resolute step he took, the chameleon's two funnel-shaped eye sockets circled in opposite directions, seeming to move independently of each other. It was clear that this little creature was blessed with 360 degree vision.

Though man is a creature with far greater intellect than a chameleon, I cannot imagine seeing in all directions and making sense of all I see in the world around me.

I remembered hearing a Bible verse when I was young, about God's eyes moving to and fro over all the earth, and so I searched for it when I returned home. The Old Testament scene is the time of King Asa, king of Judah, who obeyed God and won many battles, solely because God gave the victory. But Asa became proud and angry, so the Lord stripped him of His favor. God's eyes had no difficulty deciphering the good from evil in King Asa. He placed another king in power who would obey Him, and blessed him.

While I know that God is omnipresent and omniscient, the chameleon's eyes remind me that He takes in all the good and evil in this world at the same time. This thought blesses me for two reasons: First, I know that God seeks out those who are covered by Christ's righteousness. His eyes are moving to and fro, searching for those who are fully committed to Him. He hears their prayers and strengthens them. Second, He is just as aware of those who do not obey. He settles scores.

This is freedom for me. God has great reward for those who believe and obey Him, and those who refuse to honor Him will be punished. I don't have to worry about injustice, because my God has 360 degree vision.

> For the eyes of the LORD
> are toward the righteous,
> And His ears attend to their prayer,
> but the face of the LORD
> is against those who do evil.
> 1 Peter 3:12 (NASB)

~4~
Maasai Warrior Guardians

The LORD will protect you from all evil;
He will keep your soul. The LORD will
guard your going out and your coming in
From this time forth and forever.
Psalm 121:7-8 (NASB)

The Swahili word "Karibu" means "welcome." We were welcomed warmly at the Karibu Kirurumu Manyara Lodge, which overlooks the Great Rift Valley, and Manyara National Park. After checking in, we were led by four men dressed in the traditional red and/or blue Maasai tribal clothing, to our tented chalet. Though the inside of the chalet was quaint, with wrought-iron beds draped in cloud-soft mosquito netting canopies, it was the view out of our front door that left us breathless.

Golden hues from the late sun contrasted with the dark green colors of vegetation in the Rift Valley that spread for miles. I noticed the faint pink shade of hundreds of flamingoes in the distant Lake Manyara. We quickly settled into our tent, thrilled by the view framed by our porch's peaked rafters. It was the perfect combination of rustic and elegant styles.

I didn't notice until after dinner that the same Maasai warriors were waiting to walk us from the open-air dining room back to our chalet again. Our waiter told me that these men would be guarding outside our doorstep for the entire night. Only the strongest and bravest of young Maasai men become the warriors of their tribes, and because of this, they are often employed as night watchmen at hotels and lodges in Tanzania. Each warrior carries a staff, a knife, and a club, and is prepared to protect against any wild animal or thief they may encounter during the night. Willy told me that the lions fear the Maasai warriors, and recognizing their smell, avoid any contact with them. They are fearless.

The next morning, we zipped up our bags, and as soon as we stepped out of the chalet, our faithful Maasai warriors jumped up from their perch on a log, where, I was told, they took turns catching quick naps during the night. They helped us with our bags and escorted us to our jeep.

I needed this reminder that God is all the more reliable to watch over me. I am safe with my Warrior-Guardian God, Who never sleeps and is always there, and has promised that He will never leave me.

You will not be afraid of the terror by night...
or...the pestilence that stalks in darkness...
Psalm 91:5-6 (NASB)

In peace I will both lie down and sleep,
For You alone, O LORD,
make me dwell in safety.
Psalm 4:8 (NASB)

~5~
The Hungry Lioness

The young lions do lack and suffer hunger;
But they who seek the LORD
shall not be in want of any good thing.
Psalm 34:10 (NASB)

Two lionesses were spotted up on the grassy hill. We spied them through binoculars soon after entering the springtime-lush of Ngorogoro Crater Park. We drove on, and enjoyed viewing elephants, zebras, wildebeest, giraffes, and so many other beautiful animals. There were also countless birds: flamingos, herons, egrets, and marabou. A hyena was happy with his earlier catch—too far eaten to tell what living animal it had been, for which I was glad.

As the sun turned hotter and the shadows longer, I looked up to the hill where we had first spotted the lions. I looked through the binoculars' lens, and, in a silly way, beckoned them with crooked wiggling fingers to come closer, as if they were my house cats. To my amazement, one of the lionesses stood and trotted towards us, down the hill, to just a few feet from our safari jeep. Her mouth was agape, her eyes searching the grassy plains. Then we noticed that she was skinny—her flesh hanging from pronounced ribs. How could this be, with all the other animals in the Crater so fat and serene?

Willy explained that because the prey animals were eating well, they were strong, and so as plentiful as they were, no easy catch was to be found for a hungry, weak lioness. I pitied her, for she was a beautiful creature who also needed to feed.

I thought of our world; our culture is so alive with opportunity, education, and adventure. But the human heart has a deep hunger for more than this world can offer. If I do not feed on His Word, my spiritual flesh hangs from my spiritual ribs. I can search within the worldly walls of our culture but come back wanting. That is what the lioness did. I felt a yearning for her to eat. But for myself, I yearned for more. I want to feast on the Lord Jesus. I want to be nourished by His Word.

> [Jesus said,] "I am the living bread
> that came down out of heaven;
> if anyone eats of this bread,
> he will live forever; and the bread also
> which I will give for the life of the world
> is My flesh."
> John 6:51 (NASB)

~6~
Angry Elephant

A gentle answer turns away wrath,
But a harsh word stirs up anger.
Proverbs 15:1 (NASB)

Rattling down the gravel road, our jeep descended into Ngorogoro Crater, entering a magical African world. Bursts of yellow flowers dotted the verdant grassland, and the purple volcanic rock flushed the crater's rim in the distance. The bright sun shone on zebra stripes as they grazed and highlighted the hyena's spots as he lay in the middle of the jeep's path. It seemed we were invisible in this world. We swerved around the sunbathing hyena and then slowed to observe zebras and elephants meandering across the road.

One huge bull elephant suddenly lumbered toward us and turned to face our jeep. His tusks were long, his body huge and powerful. He stomped closer and planted himself directly in front of us. I could clearly see the flies clinging to his flapping, rough ear. It was now clear that he saw our jeep as a threat, swaying and making low grunting sounds. And we were afraid.

I had heard of elephants overturning jeeps in Africa, and I was petrified at the thought of it happening to us. Willy cautioned us to be quiet. He put the jeep in reverse, and slowly, slowly backed up several feet. The bull elephant stood motionless for a moment. The supposed threat of our jeep seemed now to be wiped from his memory. Perhaps he felt he had established his dominance. And so he turned aside, tromping away into the green and yellow fields.

In my fast-paced world, slow is not an attribute to which I normally aspire. I want to be better, faster, and more efficient. But when faced by a person as angry as a bull elephant, I am sometimes afraid and don't know how to respond. Is it a misunderstanding? Have I done something to offend? I will always remember how Willy backed away from the bull elephant in the jeep. The solution for anger is not efficiency and speed. I have learned that slowness, stillness, is effective in convincing anger to subside. I will remember to listen, not to use defensive words, and to gently and slowly respond to anger. The next time you encounter a person who is as angry as the bull elephant, try this biblical formula.

> *This you know, my beloved brethren.*
> *But everyone must be quick to hear,*
> *slow to speak and slow to anger;*
> *for the anger of man does not achieve*
> *the righteousness of God.*
> James 1:19-20 (NASB)

~7~
Nature versus Reconciliation

For all creation is waiting eagerly
for that future day when God will reveal
who his children really are.
...But with eager hope, the creation looks
forward to the day when it will join
God's children in glorious freedom
from death and decay.
Romans 8:19-21 (NLT)

God has put rules of nature in place that organize and continue the cycles of life that He has created. That is a marvel. I see it in Tanzania. Life is harsh, but it is good. Since the time that evil entered the world through the sin of man, the whole creation suffers from brokenness. I cannot avoid this reality when I see one animal give its life so that another may eat. Diseases, such as the rampant HIV and Ebola viruses and Malaria, plague our world, and man's inhumanity to man is an evil that far exceeds nature's ills and disasters.

My hope of reconciliation has always been important to me. I love people and animals, and I hate to see any of them suffer. Jesus noted that His Father sees every sparrow that falls, and so I know my God cares deeply for all His created beings as well.

In chapter eleven of Isaiah, some of the African animals are specifically mentioned in God's promises about Christ's return. Isaiah wrote that the leopard would lie down with the goat, and the lion will eat straw like the ox. When I look at the lion's and the leopard's huge flesh-tearing teeth, I do not know how God will do this, just that He will. The same God that created everything and put the world in order, is not distant from what He has made. He cares for His creation, and has a marvelous plan for every part of it.

A thought like this changes the way I look at the whole world. It changes my perception of suffering because the lens I am looking through is hope. I still hate to see God's children and creatures suffer, but I know that He will not leave it so forever. He is a God of reconciliation, meaning that He will, in His time, bring all things back under His control and glorious perfection. God is trustworthy, and when He says He will work all things out to my good, He means it, and I believe Him. Let these thoughts change the way you perceive the world also. We serve a loving, caring God, Who will reconcile all things to Himself at the appearing of our Lord and Savior, Jesus Christ. Amen.

> For it was the Father's good pleasure
> for all the fullness to dwell in Him,
> and through Him to reconcile
> all things to Himself,
> having made peace through the blood
> of His cross; through Him, I say,
> whether things on earth or things in heaven.
> Colossians 1:19-20 (NASB)

~8~
A Mighty Rock in the Desert

Let all that I am wait quietly before God,
for my hope is in him.
He alone is my rock and my salvation,
my fortress where I will not be shaken.
My victory and honor come from God alone.
He is my refuge, a rock
where no enemy can reach me.
Psalm 62:5-7 (NLT)

A month before going on safari in Africa, I was challenged in my Bible study group to memorize Psalm 62. King David wrote it, and his words still apply to me today, as they did to him the day he wrote them. Since that time, I recite it often, and sometimes one phrase stands out to me, sometimes another. Usually I find comfort in "God alone," "my victory," and "my hope is in Him." But I learned a new word in Tanzania that amplifies this scripture for me. "Kopjes" (Kop'-hees). Kopjes rise up suddenly from the mostly flat, dry grassland in the Southern Serengeti. They are huge granite boulders, sometimes stacked in a way that looks purposeful, like the formations we see at Arches National Park in Utah. They form a hill of rockery, and large shady trees and bushes somehow grow amongst them.

On our second day in the Serengeti, we hoped to see a leopard—one of the more elusive species that live there. And do you know where we found him? Atop a huge boulder on a kopje, in the shade of an acacia tree. It is true that the leopard is a preying cat, but he is still in need of a safe refuge, since no animal in the Serengeti is safe from predators. We admired his beautiful coat and his effortless agility as he moved from boulder to tree branch, up to the top of the kopje for a quick look-out, then back to the shade of the tree and the cool of the rock.

My God is like a kopje to me. The kopje's illustration gives a greater depth to the phrases, "my rock," and "my refuge." I am learning to see and hear the gentle, but extraordinary messages from God in the ordinary around me. As the leopard took refuge in the kopje, so I take refuge in God, my Mighty Rock!

> But blessed are your eyes, because they see;
> and your ears, because they hear.
> For truly I [Jesus] say to you
> that many prophets and righteous men
> desired to see what you see, but did not see it,
> and to hear what you hear, but did not hear it.
> Matthew 13:16-17 (NASB)

> Behold, I am doing a new thing!
> Now it springs forth; do you not perceive
> and know it and will you not give heed to it?
> I will even make a way in the wilderness...
> Isaiah 43:19 (AMP)

~9~
Warthog in Danger

But the Lord stood with me
and strengthened me...
and I was rescued out of the lion's mouth.
The Lord will rescue me from every evil deed,
and will bring me safely to
His heavenly kingdom;
to Him be the glory forever and ever. Amen.
2 Timothy 4:17-18 (NASB)

Willy, our safari guide, pointed out a lioness, high on the rock of a kopje, and I stood with binoculars to see her. Then in rasped whisper, he added, "Look at the warthog. The lioness sees it." I focused on the warthog in the grass, just a few meters away from where the lioness stood unflinching, alert. The warthog was unaware of any pending danger, and actually moved toward the lioness. In the tension, I didn't know whether to hope the lioness would be successful in her catch, and we would witness an exciting kill, or if I hoped the warthog would live another day. And so I waited to see how nature would steer the course. The stealthy lioness inched closer. The warthog stepped closer, his front hooves now on the base of the rock where the anticipating lioness crouched above. She seemed to beckon to him by the sheer act of her will, and he seemed helplessly drawn to her, as to a mythological siren. His nose in the air, the warthog finally caught the lioness' scent and suddenly scuttled away. The lioness pounced down from the rock, but the warthog had enough head start to narrowly escape—this time.

When I read the Apostle Peter's warning that the devil is like a lion, seeking someone for dinner, I think of the lioness and the warthog. He constantly prowls and he waits patiently for the time he might pounce or give chase. Can you remember a time when evil seemed to draw you, as you were unaware? You and I are not alone as we face evil. The Apostle Paul tells how Christ stood with him, and how he was "delivered out of the lion's mouth." Evil lurks, but there is a Savior who remains with us, and delivers us from danger if we are alert, and remain focused on Him. Trust the One Who will either guide you around, or walk through the times of unseen danger with you. You may be unaware, but He is in control. Praise God!

Be of sober spirit, be on the alert.
Your adversary, the devil, prowls around
like a roaring lion, seeking someone to devour.
1 Peter 5:8 (NASB)

~10~
Searching for the Center

*You will seek Me and find Me
when you search for Me with all your heart.*
Jeremiah 29:13 (NASB)

After a day full of lions, warthogs, giraffes, and cheetahs, I anticipated our next tented camp, and the night's rest ahead. "Kati-Kati" is the Swahili word for "center," and the Kati-Kati camp is somewhere in the middle of the huge Serengeti National Park. The word somewhere is key, because it is a mobile camp site, moved every three or four months to protect the wildlife and the environment of the park. Our guide, Willy, took us to where he thought the camp was, and—nothing was there. Unconcerned, I blissfully soaked in the sunset colors on the desert landscape. But Willy was nervous because he knew it was both unlawful and dangerous to drive the Serengeti in the dark night. After over an hour of driving, I considered the precarious night we might have to spend sitting in the parked jeep. It would be our only protection against big cats and hyenas on their night-hunts, should we not find the camp before nightfall. Willy continued to drive, also calling on his phone and CB radio to find out where the Kati-Kati camp was. Just as the last rays of light disappeared from the horizon, the Kati-Kati camp appeared before us. We were quickly escorted to a late dinner and to our tent. I was grateful for Willy's tenacity. He searched to find the Kati-Kati in the Serengeti.

King David passed this wisdom about searching for God to his son and king-to-be, Solomon, and it is my instruction as well. He said:

*As for you, my son Solomon,
know the God of your father, and serve Him
with a whole heart and a willing mind;
for the LORD searches all hearts,
and understands every intent of the thoughts.
If you seek Him, He will let you find Him;
but if you forsake Him,
He will reject you forever.*
1 Chronicles 28:9 (NASB)

I am learning that searching for God pays off in a big way. In the past, when I have ignored God, or rebelled against Him, my life eventually became disastrous. The time I take to search for God, for more of Him and to go deeper with Him, is never time wasted, and leads to my personal "Kati-Kati," a centering in God. I am still searching, and I will not give up. I know that He promises success when I seek Him with all my heart.

~11~
The Same Spirit of Faith

*And all ate the same spiritual food;
and all drank the same spiritual drink,
for they were drinking from a spiritual rock
which followed them;
and the rock was Christ.*
1 Corinthians 10:3-4 (NASB)

By the third day of our safari, we realized what a gem we had in our safari guide, Willy. He was knowledgeable, understandable (Maasai and Swahili are his first languages), and had a great sense of humor. While in the tented camp of the Serengeti, he was able to join us for dinner that night, and asked if he could say the blessing for the meal. As I listened to him pray, it took only a moment to realize that this man had a faith that was the same as mine. As we sipped our pureed vegetable soup, and hungrily feasted on cacciatore, lamb, and other dishes presented by our chefs, I looked at him as he sat across the table from me. Now I knew him as a brother in Christ, and from that point until our departure, he and I shared scriptures and spiritual encouragement with each other, as well as our personal stories of salvation. Though it's unlikely I will see him again face to face until heaven, I am praying for Willy, that he may live a life of victory in Jesus.

Our connection with other believers—those who are part of the kingdom of God—spans all time and space. We are connected to the saints of old because we believe as they did, in a Holy God, Who has a plan of redemption for His loved ones. And so are we also one church with true believers across this earth who live in distant lands and cultures, joined by our Rock and risen Lord, Jesus Christ. I find the thought of this exhilarating, since I plan on sharing my eternity with these precious souls, who are part of God's kingdom.

Whether you have had a similar experience to mine, meeting a Christian brother or sister from a different culture than your own, or felt this connection with those you have read about in the Bible, who lived thousands of years ago, try to imagine the heavenly scene of our feast in heaven. Perhaps I will be seated near one of Christ's apostles, and Willy will again be across the table from me. Jesus will sit at the head of the table, and all who are cleansed by the sacrificial blood of the Lamb, whether before or after the cross, will be there. Believers from every tribe, every language, and every nation, will be praising our God, Who is worthy to receive all praises and glory, forever and ever!

> *Worthy are You [Jesus,]...for You were slain,*
> *and purchased for God with Your blood,*
> *men from every tribe and tongue*
> *and people and nation.*
> Revelation 5:9 (NASB)

~12~
Serengeti Sunset

O LORD my God, how great you are!
You are robed with honor and majesty.
You are dressed in a robe of light.
Psalm 104:2 (NLT)

There is something about a Serengeti sunset or a sunrise. It causes a person to gaze, no matter how busy the day. All is forgotten for a moment, just to soak in its pure beauty. Trees that in the day, blend into the dry landscape, become striking silhouettes, framing the red-orange, pink-purple sky. Sunrises and sunsets are lovely bookends, set at the beginning and end of each day.

In the Serengeti, sunrise signals the end of the night-hunt, when birds twitter and bravely leave their nests, with the promise of a new day. Sunset is the quiet settling of gentle creatures seeking refuge before hyenas and lions prowl.

Sunrises and sunsets instill a sense of hope for both man and beast. They fall quietly like snow and are beautiful from every position and in every circumstance. They cover imperfections. Consider the Jewish Holocaust prisoner in a death camp yard, when a spectacular sunset descended across the sky. It would have been no less glorious to him had he lounged on the porch of his family estate. And possibly, the memory of the same brought him hope.

I think God takes great joy in painting the sky. It is His canvas used to display His glory. For followers of

Jesus, the brilliant skies arouse our expectant awe at the sight of Christ's return and the promised peace of His eternal reign. He is the Bridegroom and the Champion that is compared to the sun on its path from east to west, from the beginning of all days to the end of all days. He is Light, like a prism; full of faceted color. He is our hope.

The next time I meditate on a sun rising or setting, I will remember the glory of the Serengeti sky. Through Christ this earth was formed, and He will return again in glory. On that day His righteousness will fall like snow, covering our imperfections. He is the Prince of Peace. I anticipate His glorious coming, as He rides across the sky to His reign forever!

> The heavens are telling the glory of God;
> And their expanse is declaring
> the work of His hands.
> In them [the heavens] He has placed
> a tent for the sun,
> Which is as a bridegroom
> coming out of his chamber;
> It rejoices as a strong man to run his course.
> Its rising is from one end of the heavens,
> And its circuit to the other;
> And there is nothing hidden from its heat.
> Psalm 19:1, 4b-5 (NASB)

~13~
Colors

*So, as those who have been chosen of God,
holy and beloved, put on a heart of compassion,
kindness, humility,
gentleness and patience...
Beyond all these things put on love,
which is the perfect bond of unity.*
Colossians 3:12 & 14 (NASB)

    On the morning of our very early drive near the Kati-Kati Serengeti, our family of three piled into the jeep expectantly. Willy turned in his seat to look at us. I had a green shirt on, my husband a blue, and our daughter wore a purple and black top. "You might want to wear something different," he said. "The tsetse flies will feast on you." I remembered the big tsetse fly traps in various trees around the perimeter of the camp. They were large sheets of black and blue cloth, hung in the trees to attract tsetse flies away from our khaki tents in the Kati-Kati Camp. Tsetse flies are lured to these rich colors, and then controlled by insecticides on the cloth and caught in a bag beneath. We asked Willy what colors we should wear, and were told to clothe ourselves in light, neutral colors. Five minutes later, we climbed back in the jeep with appropriate colors, receiving an approving nod from Willy, and were on our way.
    In my everyday mornings, I get dressed,

eventually. Choosing my clothes for the day, I choose the colors I'm in the mood to wear, pairing tops with pants or a skirt, and lay out a sweater to coordinate with my outfit. I sometimes think about how the Apostle Paul challenges me to don spiritual clothing. Biblical character traits are the appropriate clothing for a follower of Jesus Christ. Compassion, kindness, humility, gentleness, and patience are the clothes I should choose, and love is the sweater to go with everything. These traits repel the spiritual tsetse fly. While I am conscientiously clothing myself, God adds the most important wardrobe component of all—power from His Own Spirit. Without the power of the Holy Spirit in me, my spiritual clothing is of little value. But God has promised to give His Spirit, and so I am confident of His presence within me.

May you and I ask for His Spirit in and over us, waiting for Him in obedience and prayer, never spiritually dressed without Him.

Dear God, thank You for showing me what to wear spiritually. Please clothe me with Your Spirit, that I may move in Your power here on earth, and wait until the day You clothe me in heaven's white robe of righteousness. Amen.

> [Jesus said] "And behold, I am sending forth
> the promise of My Father upon you;
> but you are to stay in the city until you have
> been clothed with power from on high."
> Luke 24:49 (NASB)

~14~
Bat-eared Fox

*Now therefore, if you will obey My voice in truth
and keep My covenant, then you shall be
My own peculiar possession and treasure
from among and above all peoples;
for all the earth is Mine.*
Exodus 19:5 (AMP)

In the first hours of golden desert morning light, I saw an animal which I had never seen, or even heard of. Our jeep startled the creature, and he froze for a moment, giving me long enough to clearly see his unique little face. The bat-eared fox has a droll raccoon mask, and his oversized kitten-shaped ears make his face appear small and sweet. However, he is not named for either a raccoon or a kitten, but for a bat, and so my perspective of him was not like the average biology textbook.

All the African animals are artfully designed by their Creator, but something about the bat-eared fox resonates to me that you and I are His peculiar, treasured possessions. Nothing flashy, majestic, or powerful—just unique. No other person in this world has ever had an identical relationship with God as I have, as you have. Relish this. Rest on it. The same God that created and sustains detailed microorganisms, and that has no problem maintaining a universe at the same time, is the same God that made the unique bat-eared fox, and also loves you and me. Never dwell on the thought that you are one in countless others who are loved by your Creator. Rather abide in the singularity of God and you, His one-of-a-kind treasure.

Just as God called Abraham long ago to begin a new nation that He would favor through the ages, He also called Abraham His friend. He also invites me into His heavenly kingdom, and within that kingdom of believers, He invites me to a deep and personal relationship with Him. Though I feel I am just a microorganism—a nobody; I am in truth a bat-eared fox, a unique treasured possession of my Lord and Savior, Jesus Christ. What makes the difference is how my Lord sees me. You and I are not just one of many, we are each one special in God's sight.

Let us remember today that He desires relationship with us. Let's talk to Him. Listen to Him. Learn of Him and follow Him. We will never have another relationship like it, nor will He.

> But you are... [God's] own purchased,
> special people, that you may set forth
> the wonderful deeds and display
> the virtues and perfections of Him
> Who called you out of darkness
> into His marvelous light.
> Once you were not a people [at all],
> but now you are God's people;
> ...and have received mercy.
> 1 Peter 2:9-10 (AMP)

~15~
Yellow Weaver Bird

...having been knit together in love
...resulting in a true knowledge of God's
mystery, that is, Christ Himself,
in whom are hidden all the treasures
of wisdom and knowledge.
Colossians 2:2b-3 (NASB)

The bright, industrious African yellow weaver bird thrives in the thorny branches of acacia trees. The male weaver bird's enclosed nest is a marvel of nature, and with his craftsmanship, he attracts a female. She will choose him as a mate, based solely on the quality of his nest, where she will make her home and have a family. The weaver bird's nest hangs down from the branch, like a big ornament on a Christmas tree. I had never seen anything like this unique nest before. It is anchored to the acacia branch by a single, thick, knotted grass blade. The weaver ties this knot with its beak and feet. Sometimes, his thick blade breaks, but he immediately begins again the construction of a new, stronger nest. He then weaves the additional grasses he has collected in and out, to form a safe home that swings in the gentle desert breeze.

This intricate nest reminds me of the mystery of Christ. Jesus is called a "Tender Shoot" in Isaiah 53. He is the single anchoring blade of grass that supports our everlasting salvation. It sounds precarious, doesn't it? It certainly would be, except that Christ is the Son of God, and One with God, and so His seeming "weakness" is beyond any existing human strength. The Father is like the weaver bird, planning, building, and weaving all of history and a glorious future on Christ, the carefully knotted Anchor.

The African yellow weaver bird's swinging nest illustrates the story of my eternal salvation, which rests on the sacrifice and craftsmanship of the Father, the Tender Shoot that is Jesus Christ, and the safety of what God has built for me. There is no better nest, no better Anchor.

Thank You, God, for Your masterful plan of redemption for this world. Thank You, Jesus, for Your willingness to become the Tender Shoot that is the anchor for my salvation. Thank You, Holy Spirit, for revealing to us the mystery of God's Word. Amen.

But we speak God's wisdom in a mystery...
For to us God revealed them through the Spirit;
for the Spirit searches all things,
even the depths of God.
1 Corinthians 2:7a &10 (NASB)

~16~
Majesty

*...Stop weeping; behold,
the Lion that is from the tribe of Judah,
the Root of David, has overcome...*
Revelation 5:5 (NASB)

In the golden afternoon sun, he sat upon the highest rock. His mane and coat reflected the gold in the grasses, as it ruffled with the gentle breeze. No wonder a lion is the symbol of majesty, for he exudes confidence, strength, and beauty. Every eye and camera in the four jeeps surrounding the rock was fastened upon him. He yawned, and hushed "Ooh"s and "Aah"s rose from his audience. We captured only a fragment of his majesty on film. I do not know how much time passed as we gazed upon him, for he was splendid, and for us, time stood still. He seemed to look directly at us, but gave us no attention, as if the admiration of all who viewed him was an everyday, ordinary occurrence. He was, after all, the king of beasts.

In C. S. Lewis' beloved classic series, The Chronicles of Narnia, Christ is portrayed by the great lion, Aslan. If you have read any of these books, you know how Aslan is described as both meek and powerful. He is good, but like the African lion, "not tame." Yet there is no question, Aslan is worthy of all the honor given to him. And—spoiler alert—the book ends with his subjects eagerly awaiting his return, when he will reign again.

Jesus Christ is the perfect vision of Majesty. One day, all eyes will be on Him, as He returns to claim His own. He will appear in all His glory, and it will be marvelous! I am one of His own, but when I see Him with my own eyes, I'm not sure how I will respond. Will I want to embrace Him, kneel before Him, or simply tremble at His holiness and gaze upon His splendor? When He turns His gaze toward me, I know He will look on me with love. He will dry every tear I have ever cried. I want to be one of the servants that He commends for having been "good and faithful." And I will follow Him wherever He leads, filled with the fear of the Lord, the awe of His holy perfection.

Meditate on His majesty, strength, and beauty now. Perhaps sing a song to Him, giving the glory His Name so deserves. Imagine the day you will gaze on His majestic form, as you read the Word and prepare to meet Him face to face on that glorious day.

> *They will walk after the LORD,*
> *He will roar like a lion;*
> *Indeed He will roar*
> *And His sons will come*
> *trembling from the west.*
> Hosea 11:10 (NASB)

~17~
Zebras and Hyenas

*Hate evil, you who love the LORD,
Who preserves the souls of His godly ones;
He delivers them
from the hand of the wicked.*
Psalm 97:10 (NASB)

A bulbous cloud of dust across the Serengeti alerted our safari group that something exciting was happening beyond the jeep. Upon reaching the location of the dust cloud, we saw the zebras, and it was they who were causing the dust to swirl. For a moment our view was only desert dust, with a black and white blur, and we strained to see the action in front of us. Suddenly, out of the dust cloud ran two baby hyenas, and not far behind them, two adult hyenas. Willy explained what had taken place. The zebras, ever-vigilant of their preying enemies, had seen an opportunity to stamp out future enemies. They were kicking at the hyena pups to kill them. Somehow, this time, the hyena parents distracted the zebra melee enough for the pups to escape, but many times zebras are successful in eliminating an enemy before it grows up to be a threat. I was amazed at this instinctual awareness of future danger that causes the zebras to corporately attack when their enemy is new and weak. As striking as it is to think about graceful zebras killing pups, there is an important truth in this story.

When I was in college, I met an attractive guy. I knew he was not a good influence for me, but convinced myself that he was a harmless new love. My parents, aware of the dangers, prayed constantly with Christian friends. Through their prayers, and not from my doing, I was rescued from a life of regret, when my boyfriend left on a hitch-hiking trip and I never saw him again.

God knows the enemy, just as the zebras do in the Serengeti. Satan sneaks in shrewdly, appearing as small and innocent, when we allow him to bend or stretch God's truth. If we ignore him in small things, he will increase in his lies, exercising greater control, like a fully-grown, frightful, preying hyena. But we are not helpless, nor are we left to stamp him out alone. We are offered our Lord's own armor, with which we can stave off attacks against the devil's schemes. We can put it on in confidence. Study the Word. Pray. Stand firm in your faith today.

> For our struggle is not against flesh and blood,
> but against the rulers, against the powers,
> against the world forces of this darkness,
> against the spiritual forces of
> wickedness in the heavenly places.
> Therefore, take up the full armor of God,
> so that you will be able to resist in the evil day,
> and having done everything, to stand firm.
> Ephesians 6:12-13 (NASB)

~18~
Elephant Babies

Therefore be imitators of God,
as beloved children; and walk in love,
just as Christ also loved you
and gave Himself up for us,
an offering and sacrifice to God
as a fragrant aroma.
Ephesians 5:1-2 (NASB)

Never having seen elephant families roaming in the wild before, I loved watching mama elephants care for their babies. Closer than a shadow, mirroring mama's every turn and trunk swing, the babies moved fluidly yet adhesively beside their mothers. Mama and baby both choreographed steps for the baby to nurse, or the mama to quickly shove a clump of grass into the baby's mouth, or both might stop for a relaxing scratch on nearby tree branches. God-given instinct causes many animals to learn from their parents by imitation. Those same animal parents with copy-cat babies are the parents who protect their young—even sacrificing their own lives for the life of their offspring.

One day, we drove past a family of three elephants who were walking along a winding sliver of a stream, surrounded with dry grasses on either side. The baby elephant walked behind one parent, flanked by the other. Another safari group told me they saw this same elephant family threatened by hunting lions earlier that same afternoon. They said the parents kept the baby between them, turning to face the lions, and eventually the lions gave up the hunt upon finding the parental shield impenetrable.

I had never thought of the spiritual connection between an emulating child and a protective parent until I saw the elephants in Tanzania. Elephant babies of course, trust and follow their elephant parents, as the parents protect their babies. So it should be no surprise that you and I are instructed to be imitators of God. Jesus Christ is our perfect example, as the Only Begotten Son of our Heavenly Father. God made the ultimate sacrifice of His Son to save you and me, and Jesus died to save us from eternal death. As we imitate Jesus, we are in the right place to receive the protection of the Father, like baby elephants. But unlike the elephant babies, who have God-given instinct, we must make the conscious choice to follow Christ when He calls us, and to pattern our ways after His. Only then, can we abide within His impenetrable protection and love.

*My sheep hear My voice, and I know them,
and they follow Me;
and I give eternal life to them,
and they will never perish;
and no one is able to snatch them out
of the Father's hand.*
John 10:27-28 (NASB)

~19~
Hippos in the Sun

*All discipline for the moment
seems not to be joyful, but sorrowful;
yet to those who have been trained by it,
afterwards it yields
the peaceful fruit of righteousness.
Therefore, strengthen the hands that are
weak and the knees that are feeble,
and make straight paths for your feet,
so that the limb which is lame
may not be put out of joint,
but rather be healed.*
Hebrews 12:11-13 (NASB)

The first time I saw hippos in Africa they were mostly submerged, appearing as large boulders in the water, their round ears flicking droplets of water into the sunshine. Up and down, up and down, with a quiet, gentle sloshing as they completely disappeared under the water, and soon, round faces reappearing; they were in their element. The second time I saw hippos, they were sunning themselves by the pond. Willy commented that these hippos had been too long in the sun, and I noticed the pink sunburn on their undersides and legs—parts of their bodies that remain protected when they stay in the water. Sunburn can weaken a hippo's skin and invite infection, making him easier prey for a hungry crocodile.

Do you have some element of a sensitive, sun-damaged underbelly? Selfishness, laziness in everyday work, mismanagement of time (including time spent studying the Word and in prayer), unwise words from your lips, pastimes that are not pleasing to the Lord, impatient or angry responses, or even unrestrained thoughts? No matter the reason, if you and I have not already learned discipline in these areas of our lives, we must now deal firmly with those details which are not pleasing to God. But our Lord is encouraging here. He loves you with an unshakable love. Any small victory in these mostly hidden areas of our lives produces increased peace and healing. Ask Him to show you where to begin. Listen to Him as He reveals it to you. If you know a person who can also help you to be more accountable in your effort to be disciplined, ask if they would be willing to help you, and keep a record of your successes.

Dear Lord, show me the things in my life I must change. As I read Your Word and pray, help me to listen to You. Please give me the strength to be disciplined, so that I will reap righteousness and peace, and strengthen my spiritual arms and knees, making a level path to walk ever closer to You, my Savior. Amen.

> ...show the same diligence so as to realize
> the full assurance of hope until the end,
> so that you will not be sluggish,
> but imitators of those who through
> faith and patience inherit the promises.
> Hebrews 6:11b-12 (NASB)

~20~
Baboons

All my trusted friends,
watching for my fall, say:
'Perhaps he will be deceived,
so that we may prevail against him
and take our revenge on him.'
Sing to the LORD, praise the LORD!
For He has delivered the soul of the needy one
From the hand of evildoers.
Jeremiah 20:10b & 13 (NASB)

Baboons, like all other primates, are drawn to humans. As the safari jeep glided slowly down the dirt road, through the grassy forest in Tarangire Park, I watched the baboon families that surrounded us. Mama baboons with babies clinging tight, older baboons picking insects off each other, male baboons with bright bottoms to attract desirable females—all seemed to move in slow motion along the dusty road beside us. It was the teenage baboons that climbed on the jeep's hood, feeling the metal and glass, peering at us with great interest. Catching them in very human-like positions was entertaining: relaxing on a tree branch as if it were a chaise lounge, or intense eye contact from the other side of the jeep's windshield, we enjoyed their intelligence and personalities. They have the appearance of friendliness, but Willy had words of caution, and did not allow the young baboons to climb into the jeep through the open top. He shooed them away, and sped up the jeep a bit to keep them at a distance. Later in the safari, we were told by the hotel staff to be alert for aggressive baboons. Our Mbalageti Camp had "baboon watch" in the day, in addition to the usual Maasai guards who protected us at night.

I have met people along my life's path, who I thought were friends, even thinking we had a close friendship, who did not turn out to be a friend. Our deepest emotional wounds are inflicted by those we once considered to be our friends. Friends who show interest, but then turn ugly, devious, even aggressive, are similar to the Tanzanian baboons.

There is One who understands baboons more than any other. He is the One whose friends turned their backs while He was betrayed and crucified on a cross. He is the One Friend who will never betray us. He is faithful and true. I've learned to talk to Him about my baboons. He listens. He cares. He heals. He is my Best Friend.

...I have called you friends,
for all things that I have heard from My Father
I have made known to you...
These things I have spoken to you,
so that in Me you may have peace.
In the world you have tribulation,
but take courage; I have overcome the world.
John 15:15b & 16:33 (NASB)

~21~
The Great Migration

*...And the Lord was adding to their number
day by day those who were being saved.*
Acts 2:47b (NASB)

Perhaps you've heard of The Great Migration. Many tourists come to Tanzania and Kenya with this at the top of their list of "things to see on a safari." The Great Migration is the annual, circular movement of thousands of wildebeests and zebras across the Serengeti, searching for water and greener grasses. The strongest wildebeest leads the migration. Behind him are other strong wildebeests and zebras. Weaker animals drop out of the long journey becoming vulnerable prey for big cats and hyenas.

The long line of these wandering beasts is indeed a phenomenal sight, as they run through the desert. At times, they seemed to me a formidable force by their sheer numbers and their resolve to move forward. But they are also easily spooked; their ranks often disturbed by fear, real or imaginary.

The migration is almost comical in its disorganization, and yet it is a life and death matter. It is death for those who don't continue the journey, and necessary for life for those who do. It is amazing that it even exists.

I was privileged to witness The Great Migration in Tanzania firsthand, and we sat in the jeep for long periods of time, as wildebeests and zebras charged ahead with great speed, or fell out of rank to drink in the streams or graze.

The Christian church—not a building, not a denomination, but the one that Jesus said He would build—is rather chaotic, like The Great Migration. Those who stand on its sidelines are critical of hypocrites and take note of the church's failures: misguided theology, legalism, and personal skirmishes that often cause factions and rifts in the body of believers. But God's installment of the church is a marvelous organism. This group of people coming together for no other reason than their common faith in Jesus Christ are intended to learn to grow together in love and to bring glory to God by doing so. Like a radiant bride preparing for her wedding, so the church is beautiful to God, as to a desiring, awaiting groom.

If you have the privilege of witnessing the church of God in action, count yourself blessed. If not, then ask God to show you where He wants you to be, as part of His body, the church, and begin the task of loving God by loving others. Jesus is the spiritual Leader in the church, and His purpose for it is glorious.

> *He is before all things,*
> *and in Him all things hold together.*
> *He is also head of the body, the church...*
> Colossians 1:17-18a (NASB)

~22~
A Helper

*And I [Jesus] will ask the Father,
and He will give you another Helper,
that He may be with you forever;
that is the Spirit of truth.*

John 14:16-17a (NASB)

Although God has generously given instincts and special gifts to all the African animals, He has also provided many of them with outside help from other species. Before I traveled to Tanzania, I had heard that zebras and wildebeests traverse the Serengeti together in The Great Migration. But I learned that the wildebeest has the ability to "smell" where to find water, and the zebra benefits from this instinct.

The many helpers among wild animals is amazing. The hippo has a little black bird companion called the oxbird, who not only picks his hippo-skin free of bugs and dirt, but when the hippo's sensitive skin gets sunburned and cracks open, the oxbird makes a mud pack, that is salve for healing. Any one, or number of prey animals is readily accepted to join any other group of prey animals in the deserts of Africa. I find this arrangement the most amazing of all. The wildebeest and zebra, impala, antelope, gazelle, hartebeest, topi, eland, giraffe, or ostrich can be seen grazing together in any variety of configurations. One animal alone is "lion's food," but together they are strong. And the wildebeest, oxbird, and fellow grazing animals all thrive in their symbiotic relationships with their beneficiaries.

When Jesus walked on this earth alongside His followers, whom He loved, taught, and strengthened, they were concerned when He told them that He would be leaving them to ascend into heaven. But Jesus promised another Helper to come alongside of them after He went to be with the Father.

The Holy Spirit still comes along beside us as our Paraclete today. He is just like Jesus; just like God, because He is God. He leads us to the Truth, the Living Water. He cleanses us, and heals our deepest wounds. He is always with us, because He abides within our hearts.

And this Perfect Paraclete delights in His "symbiotic" relationship with us. The Holy Spirit's purpose is to enable us to glorify Christ Jesus, and He does so powerfully and invisibly, for He is the humility of God.

> But when He, the Spirit of truth, comes,
> He will guide you into all the truth...
> He will glorify Me, for He will take of Mine
> and will disclose it to you.
> John 16:13a-14 (NASB)

~23~
My Provider

*...your Father knows what you need
before you ask Him.*
Matthew 6:8b (NASB)

I am amazed at the good gifts God has lavished on His created things in Africa. I realized that without these gifts, the plants and animals I saw in Tanzania would have little chance for survival, and observed that their instincts were perfectly crafted for each of their particular needs. God made the lion the same color as the dry grasses, so he could have a chance at catching the swiftly-running prey that is so plentiful around him. He also gives the lion patience to wait for just the right time to pounce. He makes the front-runner warthog to hold his tail erect as he runs, so followers can see the tip of his tail in the grasses that would otherwise hide him from their view, but not high enough to be easily seen by an enemy. God gives the hippo ears that fold down as he submerges under the cool water, and then wiggle up, flicking out the water as the hippo's head pops up again for air. He fashions the little dik-dik antelope with dexterity to dart so swiftly from side to side that most preying animals won't take the trouble to hunt him. And since there are so few acacia trees in the desert, God allows them to grow long thorns to protect their leaves and bark, making them less vulnerable to hungry giraffes and heavy, leaning elephants.

Jesus talked to His followers about how God

cares for the lilies of the field and the birds of the air, but He could have given innumerable examples of God's provision in His creation. And God's rich gifts are innumerable to us. He has provided us with whatever you and I need to please Him, and to live this day for His glory.

When I was a teen, I did not see my neuromuscular condition as a gift, but rather, a curse. My physical weakness does not allow me to trust my body to push itself, causing me to forfeit activites like swimming and hiking. But I have learned to trust God instead of my own body. He has often shown His strength through my weakness, as I was a teacher and a mother of four, and at times, has even given the physical strength I need in crises. But I now recognize that my spiritual strength, as well as my physical strength, is His gift to me. He chose these gifts for me, since He knows best what I need and how my life can exemplify His power.

Often we don't recognize these gifts for what they are. Perhaps even our difficulties help us to dig down deeper, thereby finding a treasured gift from God.

The LORD will continually guide you,
And satisfy your desire in scorched places,
And give strength to your bones...
Isaiah 58:11a (NASB)

~24~
The Apple of His Eye

The LORD your God is in your midst,
A victorious warrior.
He will exult over you with joy,
He will be quiet in His love,
He will rejoice over you with shouts of joy.
Zephaniah 3:17 (NASB)

It was the last full day of safari. In the northwest corner of the Serengeti we discovered that large predatory animals were hard to find. Tsetse flies made our safari drives even more difficult, as they became ravenous in the heat of the day. The night before, I was thanking the Lord for all we had seen: from the far-away rhino to the elusive leopard, plus many beautiful and varied birds. We had viewed all we had hoped to see in Africa. The only scene I wished for was to see lions in trees. We had seen many lions in the Ngorogoro Crater and the Southern Serengeti, but they were all on rocks or in the grass. And so I asked the Lord to show me lions in trees. I didn't know if that was asking for too much, after all we had seen, but I still asked, simply because I am His child, and He, my Father.

We left early that morning to see what we could before the tsetse flies set upon us. With the pop-top of the jeep open, we enjoyed the hippos and monkeys as we ate our boxed breakfasts by the shady hippo pond. After breakfast, we drove into a sea of dry straw-colored grasses as high as the hood of the car. The sun rose higher in the sky, and so the pop-top came down, and we shooed the first tsetse flies out of the jeep before masses of them could congregate. Our four pairs of eyes searched through grasses and the few trees as we drove. Then we saw them—lions in trees! Not one or two, but nine lions, two or three on the ground and the rest in trees. We spent over an hour watching them, and when we reported our adventure to those in the camp that evening, they were in awe of what we had seen. And I felt quite loved.

    Jesus talked about asking of our Heavenly Father in the seventh chapter of Matthew. He told His followers that if they could give good gifts to their children, how much more does the Father want to give good things to His children? This does not mean that we can expect to receive anything out of selfish desire, but only the gifts that God purposes are the best for our eternal benefit. The point Jesus was making is the generous simplicity of our relationship with Father-God. You and I are so blessed to be central in our Father's mind.

Keep me as the apple of the eye;
Hide me in the shadow of Your wings...
Psalm 17:8 (NASB)

~25~
The Satisfied Lions

Let them give thanks to the LORD
for His loving-kindness...
For He has satisfied the thirsty soul,
and the hungry soul He has filled
with what is good.
Psalm 107:8-9 (NASB)

They hung in the trees, legs and tails limply, lazily drooping downwards. Their heads rested on branches, and their eyes slow-blinked and closed in the rays of sun that flashed through the leaves. Their bellies hung down too, shoved to one side of a large branch. We saw the white-with-light-spots on their fat, satisfied tummies. There were nine in all. Just the sight of these lions brought me such joy. One young lioness trotted back to the mostly eaten, but still bright red carcass, a stone's throw from the two trees. Willy said the pride had eaten a big meal, and then left to drink at the nearby stream. The vultures and marabou waited for their turn, but the jackals had seniority over them. There were two hungry jackals feeding as the scavengers stood nearby, but the young lioness' return meant their time was done, and they ran to find something less threatening to eat. The lioness snacked a bit, then called to the others to eat more, but they were too sleepy and satisfied in their tree branch hammocks to respond to her, and so she returned to the shade of her tree. A male, also young, lay in the green grass under the shady tree, and we saw that his front paws were possessively poised over a smaller kill, probably a warthog. His pride and satisfaction was expressed by his posture and the shakes of his still-short mane. This would be his snack for later in the day.

After seeing the hungry lioness days before in the Ngorogoro Crater, this satisfied pride was an illustration to me of a fat and satisfied soul in communion with God. This well-fed soul feasts and drinks, and the overflow of goodness spills out for all who are hungry, standing near.

I know what it's like to be satisfied in Christ. I know how my spirit feels after a long drink of time spent with Him in prayer. It's like after Thanksgiving dinner, pushing away from the table, thinking I can't eat or drink another thing, but in a few hours, I want more again. The exception is that there's no sluggishness here. It's the excitement from hearing the Word, when God plants a new idea or direction on which I can't wait to take action.

May you and I feast to the fullness of His Word, and drink in our eternal relationship with our Heavenly Father, and truest Friend and Brother, Jesus Christ!

The afflicted will eat and be satisfied;
Those who seek Him will praise the LORD.
Let your heart live forever!
Psalm 22:26 (NASB)

~26~
Jackal

*Devote yourselves to prayer, keeping alert in it
with an attitude of thanksgiving; praying...
that God may open up to us a door for the word,
so that we may speak forth
the mystery of Christ...
making the most of the opportunity.*
Colossians 4:2-3, 5b (NASB)

The African jackal is an opportunist. When the lioness makes a kill, the jackal waits patiently while she gorges on the meat until she is thirsty. When she leaves the carcass for a drink, he takes his turn at the smorgasbord laid out before him. I saw this the day we discovered the lions in trees. Later, I saw another jackal standing in the dry field of the Serengeti. Alert, he was watching a falcon flying with a rodent in its beak. The upstart of the jeep's motor startled the bird, and it dropped the catch. In a dramatic shift, another large bird, a yellow-billed stork, swooped in and caught the rodent mid-air, leaving both the falcon and the jackal looking after their anticipated dinners with dismay. But given another day, a similar drama might swing to the jackal's favor again. He is a master at being in the right place at the right time, for he has been gifted with an opportunistic nature.

When I think of the word "opportunist," it does not usually conjure a positive impression in my mind.

However, we are instructed to be alert and ready to spring into action whenever an opportunity arises to speak the words that God has for others and to display His character. Sometimes I feel a nudge from the Spirit to speak with someone, perhaps a stranger I happen to meet, who is hurting or in need. My words may be the comfort of God to show them that they are of great value to Him. This translates into the jackal being in the right place at the right time. What happens then, you might ask? Opportunities will jump—or fly—right in front of us, and we must be ready when we discover them.

There are many examples in the Bible of spiritual opportunists. Remember the story of Rahab the prostitute, who believed God, and was alert to hide the Hebrew spies in Jericho? God wants us all to be spiritual opportunists; so be alert and ready to answer His call.

By faith Rahab the harlot did not perish along with those who were disobedient, after she had welcomed the spies in peace.
Hebrews 11:31 (NASB)

~27~
Zebra Hugs

Therefore encourage one another
and build up one another,
just as you also are doing.
1 Thessalonians 5:11 (NASB)

I love zebras—their black and white markings, unique from each other, and their gentle faces. They look as familiar as a horse in a stable, yet painted with bold stripes. We saw thousands of zebras in Tanzania, but I never got tired of them. I noticed that many times when I spotted them, they were paired in a particular position: each zebra faced another, and they criss-crossed their necks, leaning on each other. When I asked Willy about this, he told me that this embrace lets both zebras rest their heads. But more importantly is the fact that for any prey animal, there is no rest if danger is near. And so one zebra looks one way, and the other zebra looks the other way. If a lion is stalking, one of the zebras will see it, and warn the other.

This version of a zebra hug is the way Christians should be for each other, because part of encouraging is also looking out for each other. These two components complete the picture of encouragement: to strengthen or build each other up, and to look out for each other, which leads to rest and peace, the end result of true encouragement.

The Christian life was never meant to be lived in solitude. The apostle Paul wrote often to his little churches in Asia and Macedonia, encouraging them to love and support one another, and in the book of Hebrews, he adds that this is important, especially as we see the Day approaching. That "Day" is the Day of Christ's appearing. I do think we can see that it is nearer, as recent history lines up just as prophecy has foretold. And so what are we doing as we see Christ's return coming closer? The answer is that we are encouraging, supporting, and looking out for one another's needs all the more. With like-minds of Christ, we pray for others, listen to, do for, and build up our fellow Christians.

Dear Lord, may I be ready to encourage someone today, with the same encouragement You have given me. Help me to remember the two-fold purpose in a zebra hug. Amen.

> And let us not neglect our meeting together,
> as some people do,
> but encourage one another,
> especially now
> that the day of his return is drawing near.
> Hebrews 10:25 (NLT)

~28~
Crossings

When you go through deep waters,
I will be with you.
When you go through rivers of difficulty,
you will not drown.
When you walk through the fire of oppression,
you will not be burned up;
the flames will not consume you.
Isaiah 43:2 (NLT)

When I planned our safari in the late spring, which is Southeast Africa's rainy season, I realized the possibility of torrential down-pour. And though the raingear never left our suitcases, we saw the effects of rain from the week before we arrived in Tanzania. Tarangire's shady trees were healthy and lush, and the green grasses long. The marshy waters surrounding brimming Manyara Lake attracted thousands of flamingos and other waterfowl. Ngorogoro Crater was filled with bright yellow flowers. Even the usually dry Serengeti showed signs of recent rain.

One day, while looking for a crocodile in the Serengeti, our jeep came to a crossing that looked impassable. The bridge looked like the edge of a dam, the meandering stream overflowing it, and it didn't even look like a road anymore. "This is the only way over it," Willy said, and so he carefully proceeded to cross. The water came almost to the top of the jeep's heavy tires, and for a moment, it seemed we might be swept off the road. Steadily, Willy drove through the channel of water and up onto the dry land again.

Glancing behind us, the river didn't look quite so foreboding. Why? Because we had made it through to the other side, and we were again on the road to find our crocodile.

Every life has difficult crossings at some point along the path. The way appears impassable, but with no other alternative, we cross anyway, and ask God to help us through the water, through the fire. He has promised to walk with us, even if we walk through the shadow of death.

Back-glancing is important too. God wanted His people to remember how He helped them to cross the overflowing Jordan River. The people were instructed to pile stones as a reminder, to tell the story of how God crossed with them.

I remember difficult crossings, some are so fresh that I have not yet reached the shore, and some are now a distant story, both revealing God's presence and provision.

When your children ask their fathers
in time to come, saying, 'What are these stones?'
then you shall inform your children, saying,
'Israel crossed this Jordan on dry ground.
For the LORD your God dried up the waters of the
Jordan before you until you had crossed'
...that all the peoples of the earth may know that the
hand of the LORD is mighty,
so that you may fear the LORD your God forever.
Joshua 4:21b, 22, 23a, & 24 (NASB)

~29~
Desert Streams

The wilderness and the desert will be glad,
And the Arabah will rejoice and blossom;
...They will see the glory of the LORD,
the majesty of our God.
...For waters will break forth in the wilderness
And streams in the Arabeh.
Isaiah 35:1a, 2b, 6b (NASB)

I don't think a Christian can visit the Serengeti without thinking of Isaiah's reference to the "streams in the desert." I thought of it the day we visited the hippo pond. All was dry as we set out on a safari drive, and I remember wondering how hippos could live in such an arid environment. But the streams that twist and wind through the desert are surrounded with lush green plants and even a few palm trees. Once we arrived at the hippos' home, it was a different world. Water seemed plentiful, and monkeys and birds made it their home also.

I considered another faucet to the desert streams the day we flew across the parks in a small plane on our last day in Tanzania. From the air, it's easy to see where the streams in the desert run, by the dark green color in contrast to the light yellow of the desert terrain. It's clear that the further away from the springs, the dryer the land.

One of the last hippos I saw in the Serengeti was

far from the streams and hippo pond. As our jeep bumped over the gravel road, the hippo was on a parallel path several meters away. He was actually walking away from the stream, and we noticed a trickle of blood behind, as he plodded along. I asked Willy where the hippo was going, and he told me, "I don't know, but he is in trouble."

I get it now. When I walk away from the life-giving streams, I am a hippo in trouble. I am vulnerable. I am suffering.

Restoration and refreshment? Yes, Lord, the streams of Living Water give me that. But life. I cannot live without the life and security in Your desert streams. There is no other place for me.

> Blessed is the man who trusts in the LORD
> And whose trust is the LORD.
> For he will be like a tree planted by the water,
> That extends its roots by a stream
> And will not fear when heat comes;
> But its leaves will be green,
> And it will not be anxious in a year of drought
> Nor cease to yield fruit.
> Jeremiah 17:7-8 (NASB)

~30~
Co-Pilot

*And do not be conformed to this world,
but be transformed
by the renewing of your mind,
so that you may prove what the will of God is,
that which is good and acceptable and perfect.*
Romans 12:2 (NASB)

    Though our family trio was sad to leave Willy, the safari guide we had grown to love, and the beauty and adventure of Tanzania, it was time to go. And so we boarded the small plane that would carry us from the northwest corner of the Serengeti to Arusha, from where we would fly home. Beginning our travel at the little Cessna's furthest point on its route, we were three of the five passengers on board. My husband sat down in the last row of seats beside me, but quickly spied the colorful, lighted instrument panel only four rows ahead in the cockpit. Since take-off time wasn't for a few minutes, he unbuckled and moved up front to talk to the pilot, who invited him to sit beside him as co-pilot during the flight. My husband has some flying experience with small planes, and so he was like a little boy who had just received a personal invitation to a toy store. He flashed a smile back toward me, and I knew this was the perfect ending for his safari. He watched the pilot carefully, asking questions about the flight, the pilot's experience, and the many instruments in front of them.

    I thought about God as the Pilot of my life. I have already asked Him to take control, so there is no question that He is in the pilot's seat. As I sit beside my Savior, Jesus, with the array of choices before me, I watch Him carefully, and ask Him questions about the flight before us. He is as eager to have me beside Him, as am I to be His co-pilot. There are many things I must learn about the choices on my instrument panel. I am learning how to pray more effectively. I ask Him to show His will for me—the good works He has planned for my life, since before I was born. He points to my instruments: my understanding of His Word, other godly influences He has placed in my life, and the still, small voice that speaks to my own spirit. He has given me the route to fly with Him. I am not afraid, for He is beside me, and He knows what He's doing.

> *For it is God who is at work in you,*
> *both to will and to work*
> *for His good pleasure.*
> Philippians 2:13 (NASB)

> *I press on toward the goal*
> *for the prize of the upward call*
> *of God in Christ Jesus.*
> Philippians 3:14 (NASB)

Special Thanks to:

Access 2 Tanzania Safari Tours
&
Willy Philemon
Safari guide and friend

~

Shelley L. Houston & Gayle Carlson
Whose help and encouragement has been invaluable

~

And none would be possible without the love of
my family & my Lord

CPSIA information can be obtained at www.ICGtesting.com
Printed in the USA
LVOW01s1006051114

412034LV00010B/14/P